Needle Crafts 8

THE BASIC TECHNIQUES OF
BOBBIN LACE

G000256145

SEARCH PRESS
London & New York

Introduction

Lace developed from a finishing technique used on the warp threads left over after weaving a length of cloth. At first these thread ends were knotted making a fringe that added extra length to the piece of cloth. Bobbin lace probably derived from this use of warp ends, eventually becoming independent of a loom. Lace is first mentioned in 15th Century Italian documents, and gradually developed into an intricate and exquisite craft valued all over the world.

This book is an introduction to the basic techniques of lace-making. It explains how to make a pillow, wind bobbins, prick out patterns and work three simple stitches. Full instructions are given for working cloth stitch, whole stitch and half stitch, progressing to plaits, woven bars, insertions and a narrow edging.

Today, lace techniques are used more and more in creative textile designs, and the photographs show some of the ways they can be applied. To make traditional lace, it is necessary to refer to specialized text books, but the information in this book gives enough instruction to make simple lace and any of the items illustrated.

Fig. 1 (a) Hand made hawthorn bobbin with buttons; *(b)* turned wooden bobbin ; *(c)* old bobbin with hand-made glass beads; *(d)* bobbin with sliding cover to protect the thread when working out of doors.

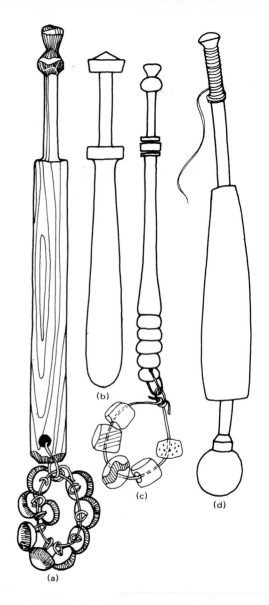

(a) (b) (c) (d)

Equipment

Pins

Fine stainless steel pins can be bought from most haberdashery stores. Mapping pins or berry-headed pins are useful for keeping bobbins not in use from rolling in among the ones being worked.

Bobbins

These are pieces of wood between 3½ and 4½ in. (9-12 cm) in length, on to which the thread is wound for easy handling while working the stitches. Old bobbins were made from ivory, brass or pewter, (fig. 1) although originally they were all made from bone and wood.

Commercially-made bobbins can be expensive but there are a number of ways in which they can be made at home.

Quarter-inch dowelling from a timber merchant can be sawn into 4½ in (12 cm) lengths, whittled into shape with a pen-knife and then smoothed down with fine sandpaper, as fig. 2.

With the help of a lathe attachment on an electric drill a handyman can turn bobbins in much less time than it takes to carve them. Woodwork teachers at local schools often prove to be a good source of supply, and rehabilitation centres often have wood-turning facilities.

As a temporary measure, pencils may be used, with the wood shaved away at one end to form a neck.

For the basic lace stitches, bobbins are used in pairs and are wound with one length of thread as shown in fig. 5.

Some types of bobbins have a hole pierced in the base through which a wire ring is passed. Square-cut beads are threaded on the ring, and there is often a larger bead at the bottom. The ring and the square-cut beads help to keep the bobbin in its place. The beads are sometimes referred to as *spangles*.

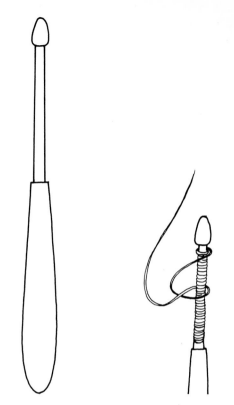

Fig. 2. A wooden bobbin.   Fig. 3. A half hitch knot.

Winding a bobbin is done by holding it in the right hand, and with the thread passing between the finger and thumb of the left hand, winding it around the neck of the bobbin in such a way as to cover all the spool.

Wind the thread tightly, as loose winding causes the bobbin to slip while working. When enough thread is wound on to the first bobbin, it is secured with a half hitch knot (fig. 3).

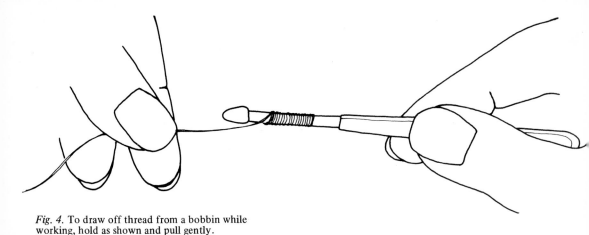

Fig. 4. To draw off thread from a bobbin while working, hold as shown and pull gently.

Do not cut the thread off, but unwind the same length of thread from the ball for the second bobbin of the pair, and then cut the thread. Starting with the cut end, wind the second bobbin as in fig. 5.

The length of thread between the two bobbins should be about 15 cm. Secure the second bobbin with a half hitch knot as before.

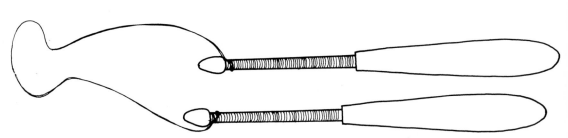

Fig. 5. A pair of bobbins wound ready to hang on a pin.

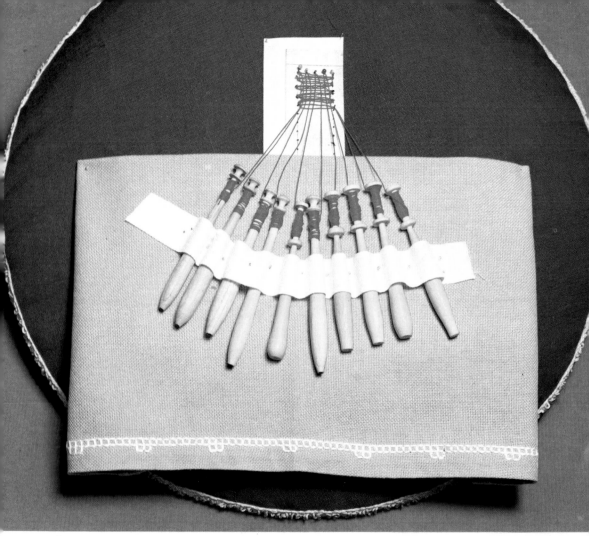

Lace pillow. The bobbins are secured with a band of fabric to prevent their tangling while not in use. The first pricking is in the process of being worked (Ziaen Lovesey, aged 7).

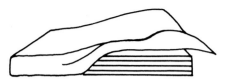

Fig. 6. Square pillow. Four polystyrene tiles 18 in. (46 cm) square, glued together and covered in dark material.

Lace pillows

These are cushions on which the lace is worked. They must be made of a substance soft enough to pierce with a pin, yet firm enough to hold the pin steady. Good lace cannot be made on a soft cushion. A simple pillow can be made from tiles of polystyrene 18 in (46 cm) square and 1-2 in. (3-5 cm) thick (fig. 6). This can be covered with a piece of dark, plain material to form a good, inexpensive base to start with. A square of fibreboard lasts quite a few months before being ruined by too many pin pricks.

A mushroom pillow can be made from two circles of calico about 45 cm diameter, machined together to form a pillowcase. This is then filled with chopped-up straw packed very tightly. The pillow is then laid on to a piece of board of the same diameter, and pinned down all round the edges to hold it firmly. Now take a piece of dark fabric 5-8 cm larger all round, and turn a hem on it wide enough to take a length of tape. Thread the tape into the hem, lay over the pillow and board, turn upside down and draw the tape up tightly. This cover should be a dark fabric to prevent eye strain when working (fig. 7).

Pincushions

Apart from the pins to be used in the pricking, it is not advisable to leave spare pins stuck in the pillow. A tradition among lace-workers has been to have a pincushion attached to the top of the pillow by a small loop.

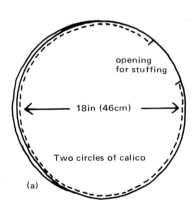

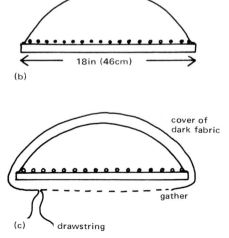

Fig. 7. Mushroom pillow. *(a)* Two circles of calico sewn together leaving a hole for the stuffing; *(b)* stuffing with chopped straw and stapling or tacking on to a circular board; *(c)* covering with a dark cloth.

Prickings

Lace patterns are called prickings, and consist of dots on stiff card showing the positions of pinholes, with a few lines indicating the directions of the threads. They can be bought commercially, or acquired from lace-makers, teaching centres or specialist magazines. To make prickings, a strong, shiny, brown card can be bought for this purpose. Alternatively stiff, brown paper or even postcards can be used.

To transfer the prickings from this book, the most simple method is to trace them on to tracing paper, then lay the tracing over card or brown paper, and pin both together on the pillow. As the pricking is worked, pins are inserted and form a permanent pricking on the card beneath. The tracing paper is only used once. Another method is to lay the tracing on card, lay both on a cork or similar surface, prick through the pattern with a lace pricker and then ink in the pattern. An item called a *pin vice* can be bought for this purpose. A pricker can be made from a sewing needle inserted into a wooden handle or a broken bobbin (fig. 8).

Terms used in the instructions

Cover the pin: Make one complete stitch with the same pair of threads round the pin, before continuing to the next pin hole.
Footings: The straight edge of the lace attached to the material. (In insertion lace, both sides are footings).
Grounds: Different types of net.
Headings: The outside edge of the lace.
Pin up: Place a pin in the pricking where the stitches are made, as indicated.
Passives: Bobbins which do not change position during working.
Pricking: The paper pattern with holes, on which the lace is made.

Set up a pillow: Pin the pricking in place and hang up the bobbins prior to starting work.
Twist: Always means passing the right bobbin over the left one.
Workers: Bobbins which are moved across the pricking to make the stitches.

Fig. 8. A pricker.

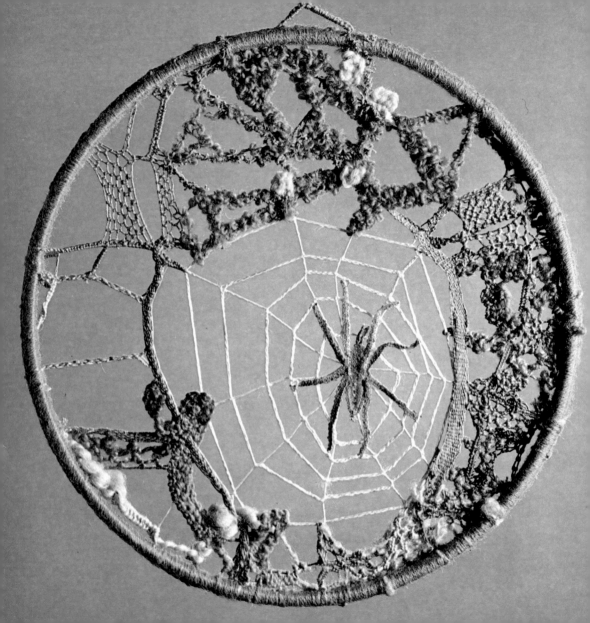

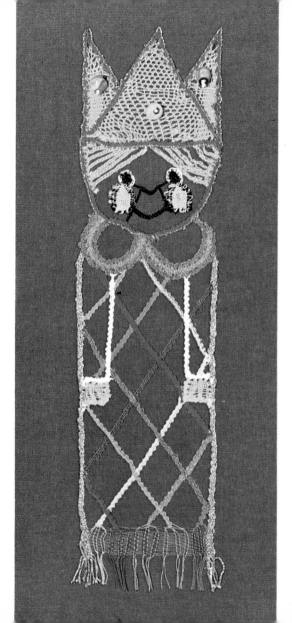

'Spider and web'. Worked on a lampshade ring in different wools. The spider is in cloth stitch, the web is made of plaits, and the tree trunks are worked in fine silk cloth stitch (Nenia Lovesey).

'Clown'. A design worked for a Duke of Edinburgh award in crochet cotton and perlé threads (Carol Townsend).

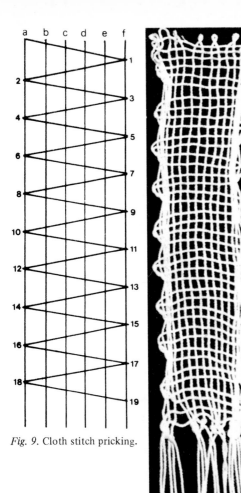

Fig. 9. Cloth stitch pricking.

Cloth stitch sample.

Starting to make lace

Cloth stitch (whole stitch)
The pricking shown in fig. 9 makes the sample of cloth stitch, shown in the photograph beside it. Cloth stitch is made by passing one pair of bobbins called the *workers* through all the other pairs called the *passives* in turn, and then back again.

Fig. 10 is a diagram of the cloth stitch sample. The first pair of bobbins are the workers, and they interlace across all the other pairs of threads to the right. At the end of the row they are twisted round a pin, and then worked back to the left.

The stitch that weaves these worker bobbins across and back is called whole stitch, and is worked with two pairs of bobbins. The first pair, which are the workers, pass through each pair of passives in turn across the row.

Working the cloth stitch sample
(1) Make a pricking (fig. 9). Trace off the pricking on to a piece of tracing paper. Place this over a piece of card.
(2) Select a thread. The sample shown is worked with crochet thread no. 40. Crochet cotton has a good twist and works well for simple lace. For different effects in lace, a variety of threads can be tried such as linen, fine wool or metal thread, but use a smooth yarn to begin with, and make sure it will wind easily on to the bobbins.
(3) Wind the bobbins. Eight pairs of bobbins will be needed for this sample. Using the chosen thread, wind one metre on to each bobbin as shown on page 4. Leave about 15 cm of thread between each pair, and secure the threads to the bobbins with a half hitch knot as in fig. 3.
(4) Set up a pillow. Pin the pricking in position. Use a pin in each corner and push each one right down to the head to avoid catching threads.

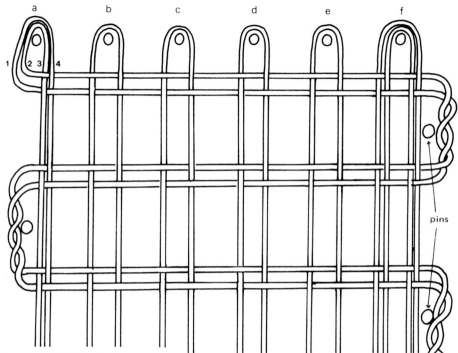

Fig. 10. Diagram of the cloth stitch sample.

Place a pin at all points marked a, b, c, etc. at the top of the pricking. Hang two pairs of bobbins at pin a, one pair on b, c, d and e and two pairs at f.

The first pair on the left are the workers, all the rest are passives.

(5) *Learn the first stitch.* Whole stitch is made by using a pair of workers and a pair of passives in four movements. Start with the first two pairs hanging on pin a and work as follows:

Number the places where the bobbins lie 1, 2, 3 and 4. These numbers refer to the *places* and not to the bobbins themselves.

It will help to memorize the following:

2 over 3
2 over 1
4 over 3
2 over 3

The sequence of moving the bobbins to make one stitch is shown in fig. 11.

Do each of the movements in the sequence separately at first. Once this is mastered it is quite simple to execute two movements simultaneously as follows:

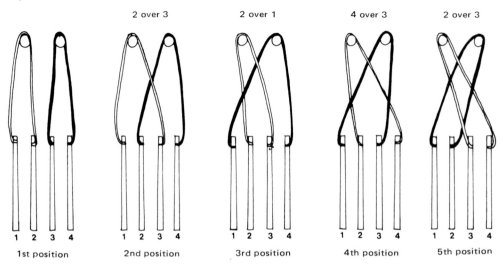

| 1st position | 2 over 3 2nd position | 2 over 1 3rd position | 4 over 3 4th position | 2 over 3 5th position |

Fig. 11. The sequence of moving the bobbins to make one stitch.

Pick up the bobbin in place 2 with the right hand, lift over the bobbin in place 3.

With the left hand, pick up from place 2 and pass over place 1, while at the same time with the right hand, pick up from place 4 and pass over place 3. The right hand picks up 2 and passes over 3 to complete the stitch.

Two pairs of bobbins are always in use at one time. Some people find it easier to work with a pair of bobbins in each hand, while others prefer to work with the bobbins lying on the pillow.

(6) *Continue to work a whole stitch* (all four movements) with the workers and the pair of bobbins on *b*, then work through *c, d, e,* and both pairs on *f.*

(7) *Turning round at the end of the row.* When the workers are on the right-hand side of *f*, take a pin and place it between the last pair at *f* and the workers. Twist the workers twice, right over left.

(*Twist,* in lace-making terms, always means passing the right bobbin over the left one). The workers then return to point 2 on the pricking.

Always remember that no matter whether workers are moving from right to left or left to right, the places in which the bobbins lie remain the same. So that when the workers reach the right side of the pricking and are pinned into position ready to return, the last four bobbins still remain in places 1, 2, 3 and 4. The workers started in places 1 and 2 when working from the left, but are now in places 3 and 4 when working from the right. Even so the movements of the stitch always remain the same.

(8) *Complete the sample* by continuing to pass the workers back and forth in whole stitches down to the bottom of the pricking, twisting at each side. To fasten off, tie threads in pairs with an overhand knot.

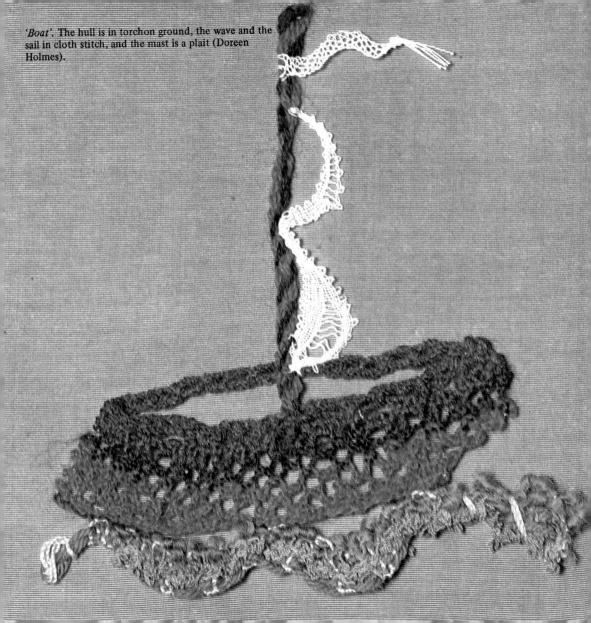

'Boat'. The hull is in torchon ground, the wave and the sail in cloth stitch, and the mast is a plait (Doreen Holmes).

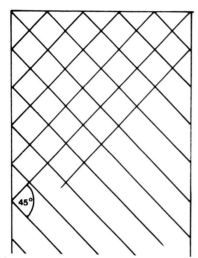

Fig. 12. Diagonal lines drawn for a Torchon ground.

Torchon ground (whole stitch)

The second sample is a strip of Torchon ground, based upon whole stitch. Although half stitch is often used as a grounding for Torchon lace, the threads tend to shift when worked by beginners, and for this reason a whole stitch ground is used here.

Unlike cloth stitch, Torchon ground is worked diagonally. The threads meet at an angle of 45° as shown in fig. 12. Angles of 45° are made by drawing diagonal lines within a square from the top right to bottom left, and from top left to bottom right, giving a series of crosses. The point where these lines cross is where the pins are inserted into the pricking.

Working the Torchon ground sample

(1) Make a pricking. Trace off the pricking (fig. 13) and pin to the pillow.

(2) Select a thread. The sample shown is worked with crochet thread no. 40.
(3) Wind the bobbins. Twelve pairs of bobbins will be needed. Wind one metre of thread on to each bobbin.
(4) Set up a pillow. Pin the pricking in position. Place a pin at *a, b, c, d,* and *e.* Hang three pairs of bobbins at *a,* two pairs at *b, c, d* and three pairs at *e.* The two pairs at *a* and *e* will be passives as in cloth stitch.

Work as follows:

(1) Take the first pair, work through the next 2 pairs.
(2) Now take a pair from *b,* and work a whole stitch with the workers from *a.* Place a pin at 1, between the two pairs, and work another whole stitch with these pairs, and cover the pin.
(3) Take the second pair from *b* with one pair from *c* and work another whole stitch. Place a pin at 2, and work another whole stitch to cover the pin.
(4) The second pair from *c* and the one pair from *d* are worked in the same way.
(5) Take the last pair at *e* and work two whole stitches to the left, and with this pair make a whole stitch with the remaining pair at *d,* pin up at 4, and make one stitch to cover the pin.
(6) The left-hand pair hanging on the pin at 1 then works out to the left through the two outside passives. Twist the threads by passing the right hand bobbin over the top of the left one *twice.*
(7) Pin up and work back through the two passives to hang on the right of these two pairs where they are worked with a pair from 1 to make one stitch at 5.
(8) Take the other pair from 1 and make a stitch with a pair from 2. Pin up and make a stitch to cover the pin at 6.
(9) Take the workers from 5 and a pair from 6 to work a whole stitch at 7.

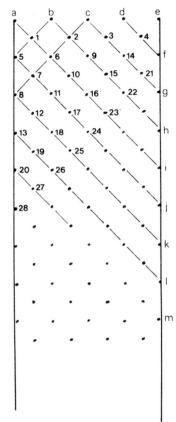

Fig. 13. Torchon ground pricking.

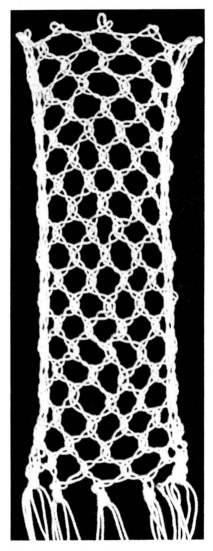

Torchon ground sample.

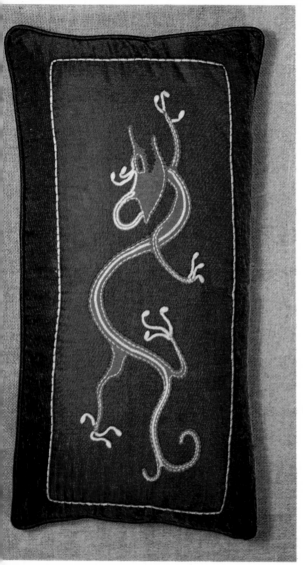

'Dragon' Cushion. A sampler of different lace techniques mounted on furnishing fabric, made from knitting and crochet yarns (Isabel Elliott).

Collar with beads. Worked entirely in cloth stitch, extra bobbins were added to increase the width, and cut out later when width diminished. The beads hang from plaits, held in place with overhand knots (Nenia Lovesey).

Hanging. Made of handspun wool in natural shades with a glint of fine gold lurex. The lace was made on the polystyrene pillow directly on to squared paper. Hand spun wool is difficult to use as the rough texture prevents the threads slipping into place, so each stitch must be positioned before moving to the next (Dorothea Nield).

Triple wall-hanging. These three braids are worked from the simple insertion pricking in wools of differing textures. A similar braid could be used to trim a wool dress, or in 40 crochet cotton could be an insertion for table linen (Isabel Rampton).

One pair from 7 works out through the two passives on the left, is given two twists as before, pinned up at 8, worked back through the two pairs of passives and left hanging.

(10) Take a pair from 2 and 3 and work 9. Then 10 is worked with pairs from 6 and 9. 11 is worked with pairs from 7 and 10. 12 is worked with the workers from 8 and a pair at 11. A pair from 12 works out through the passives, is twisted twice pinned up and worked back through the two pairs of passives and left at 13. Take the pairs at 3 and 4 to work 14 and continue down through 15, 16, 17, 18 and 19 and out through passives, twist, pin up and work back through the passives and leave at 20.

(11) The pair hanging at 4 works out to the right through the two passives at *e*, is twisted twice, pinned up and worked back through the passives at *f*.

(12) Take the pair at 14 and with the workers from *f* work 21, then down through 22, 23, 24 and 25 and on to 28.

(13) Work out through the passives, twist twice, pin up and work back through the passives and leave hanging.

Start each row at the highest point by taking the third pair in from the right, out through the passives hanging from pin *e* then working down at the 45° angle to the passives on the left-hand side hanging from pin *a*.

The whole stitch ground and the cloth stitch form the basis for much of the creative work shown in the illustrations.

Half stitch ground

At the beginning of this Century, this ground was known as *Hawkers lace,* because it was sold from door-to-door by gipsies. It was quick to make and cheap to produce and marks the start of the decline in the quality of bobbin lace design. It does not wear very well as the threads shift when washed. Nowadays it is used extensively in creative lace.

Working the half stitch sample

Trace off the pricking (fig. 14), and pin to the pillow. Twelve pairs of bobbins will be needed. Wind one metre of crochet cotton no. 40 on to each bobbin. Half stitch is worked as follows:

2 over 3
2 over 1
4 over 3

(1) Place a pin at *a, b, c, d* and *e.*

(2) Hang up three pairs at *a,* two pairs at *b, c, d* and three pairs at *e.*

(3) The left-hand pair at *a* will work through the two passives at *a* to make a half stitch with the left-hand pair at *b.* (2 over 3, 2 over 1 and 4 over 3).

(4) Pin up at 1.

(5) Cover the pin with another half stitch. This leaves each pair of bobbins twisted once.

(6) The right-hand pair at *b* and the left-hand pair at *c* will make the next half stitch.

(7) The sequence then follows the working of Torchon ground.

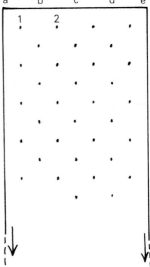

Fig. 14. Half stitch pricking.

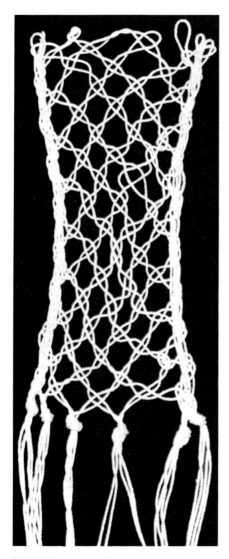

Half stitch sample.

The plait

The plait in figs. 15a and 15b is made from a continuous braid of half stitches (2 over 3, 2 over 1, and 4 over 3) for as long as necessary. This is useful to outline part of a design, or for joining two parts of a pattern together.

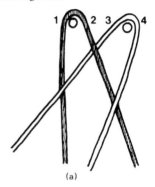

(a)

Fig. 15 (a, b). Plaiting.

(b)

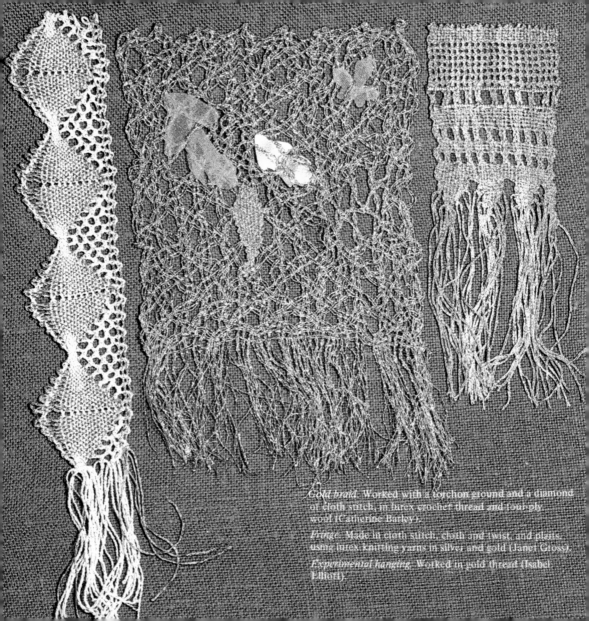

Gold braid. Worked with a torchon ground and a diamond of cloth stitch, in lurex crochet thread and four-ply wool (Catherine Barley).

Fringe. Made in cloth stitch, cloth and twist, and plaits, using lurex knitting yarns in silver and gold (Janet Gross).

Experimental hanging. Worked in gold thread (Isabel Elliott).

Braids. A selection of insertions in different threads, and in the foreground a bracelet in elastic and lurex crochet thread. (Isabel Elliott).

A woven bar

This will prove most useful in creative lace. The instructions for working are as follows:

(1) Take two pairs of bobbins and hang from one pin if a leaf shape is needed, or hang one pair from each of two pins if a square shape is needed. (fig. 16).

(2) Of the four threads now hanging, three are passives and the fourth weaves or darns under and over these passives.

(3) The thread from the weaver bobbin needs to be longer than the other three threads.

(4) Take the bobbin lying in place 2, pass it over 3, under and back over 4, then under 2, over and back under 1 (fig. 17).

(5) Continue in this way until the required length is reached.

(6) Never allow the weaving bobbin to drop or pull the other threads too tight, or the shape will be lost.

(7) By spreading the two outside threads, the weaving thread will be pushed up to make a firm woven bar.

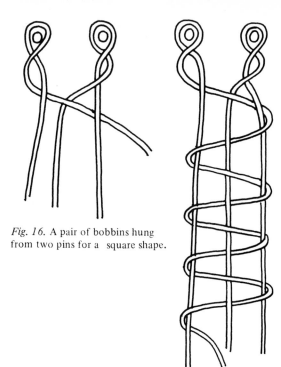

Fig. 16. A pair of bobbins hung from two pins for a square shape.

Fig. 17. Weaving pattern for a square shape.

Three woven bars can be joined together to form a leaf spray (fig. 18).

(1) Work each bar with two pairs of bobbins hung from one pin for each leaf.

(2) Shape the leaf by pulling the two outside bobbins apart toward the centre of the leaf, and drawing close together again at the base.

(3) Plait the sets of bobbins by taking the centre two pairs over the two pairs on the left.

(4) Then take the two new centre pairs over the two pairs on the right.

(5) Continue to make three more woven bars if a flower shape is needed. This will make a daisy-type shape with six petals.

Fig. 18. A leaf spray formed by three woven bars joined together.

Insertions

These are useful for threading ribbon through. An insertion is made up from two cloth stitch edges joined with whole stitch as can be seen in fig. 19. Make a tracing of fig. 20. Pin it to the pillow. Six pairs of bobbins will be needed. Wind one metre of cotton no. 10. on to each bobbin.

(1) Hang three pairs of bobbins from three pins on each side.

(2) The first pair are the workers on the left side. Work three rows of cloth stitch through the two pairs of passives. Leave at the centre.

(3) The last pair of bobbins are the workers on the right side. Work three rows of cloth stitch through the two pairs of passives. Leave at the centre.

(4) Work one whole stitch in the centre with both pairs of workers. Pin up. Make another whole stitch to cover the pin.

(5) Work six rows of cloth stitch each side to bring the workers back to the centre again. Repeat steps (4) and (5) until work has reached the required length.

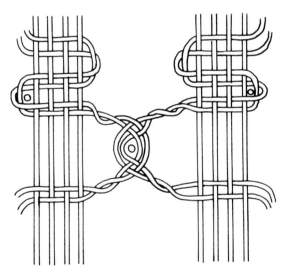

Fig. 19. Insertion made up from two cloth stitch edges joined with whole stitch.

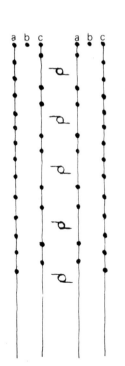

Fig. 20. Insertion pricking.

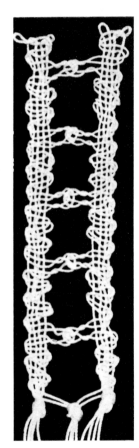

Insertion sample.

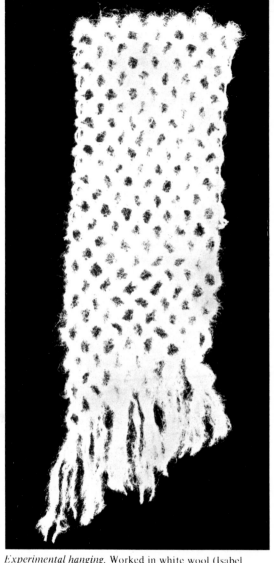

Bag. Torchon ground, using linen thread and dishcloth cotton (Janet Gross).

Experimental hanging. Worked in white wool (Isabel Elliott).

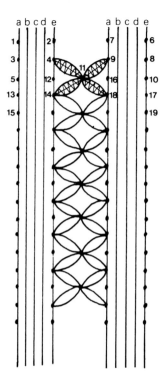

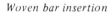

Fig. 21. Woven bar insertion pricking.

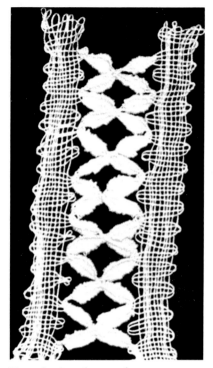

Woven bar insertion sample.

Woven bar insertion

Trace off the pricking (fig. 21), and pin to the pillow. Twelve pairs of bobbins will be needed. Wind one metre of cotton no. 60 on to each bobbin. This insertion needs five pairs of passives, one pair of workers and two pairs for the woven bar *a, b, c, d* and *e* for each side. Work it as follows:

(1) Take the workers from 1. Work in cloth stitch through to 2 and pin up.

(2) Work back to 3 and pin up.

(3) Work through to 4 and pin up. Hang the pairs for the woven bar on the pin and work through these two pairs with the workers. Remove the pin from 4 and put it back in the same hole but on the right-hand side of the two new pairs.

(4) Work back through these two pairs and on through the passives. Pin up at 5 and leave.

(5) Take the workers from 6 and work through to 7 and pin up.

(6) Work back to 8 and pin up.

(7) Work back to 9 and hang the two pairs on the

25

pin as before. Work through these, remove the pin and replace it on the left-hand side of the two new pairs and work back to 10.

(8) With the two new pairs hanging at 4, make a woven bar and pin up at 11.

(9) Repeat with the two new pairs at 9.

(10) There are now eight pairs hanging at 11. Make a whole stitch using two bobbins instead of one bobbin for each movement.

(11) With two pairs hanging on the right-hand side, make another woven bar and hang over a pin and leave.

(12) With two pairs hanging on the left-hand side, make another woven bar and hang over a pin as before.

(13) Take the workers left at 5, work through to 12, pin up, and work back to 13.

(14) Work back to 14 through the two pairs of the woven bar, pin up, and work back to 15.

(15) Take the workers left at 10, work through to 16, pin up, and work back to 17.

(16) Work through to 18, through the two pairs of the woven bar, pin up, and work back to 19.

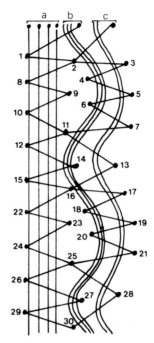

Fig. 22. Narrow edge pricking.

A narrow edging

Trace off the pricking (fig. 22), and pin to the pillow. Eleven pairs of bobbins will be needed. Wind one metre of crochet cotton nos. 40 or 60 on to each bobbin.

(1) Hang four pairs at *a*.

(2) Hang three pairs of passives and one pair of workers at *b*.

(3) Hang two pairs of passives and one pair of workers at *c*.

(4) The workers at *b* work through all the pairs to 1, pin up, and work back through the passives from *a* to 2 and are left.

(5) Take the workers from *c* and work through all pairs to 2. Make one whole stitch with the workers from *a*, pin up at 2 and cover the pin.

(6) The right-hand pair at 2 works through 3, 4, 5, 6, 7 and through to 11 and is left.

(7) The pair still at 2 works back through 8, 9, 10, to 11 and makes a whole stitch with the pair from 7. Pin up at 11 and cover the pin. cover the pin.

(8) The right-hand pair at 11 works through to 13 and is left.

(9) The pair left at 11 now works out to 12, through to 14, then 15 and down to 16 and is left.

(10) The pair from 13 works through to 16 and

26

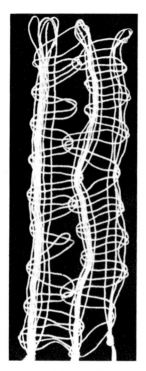

Narrow edging sample worked without twists.

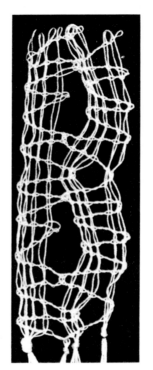

Narrow edging sample with two twists added between each pair of passives and three twists added in the space between lines of passives.

makes a whole stitch with the pair already hanging from 15. Pin up at 16 and cover the pin.

(11) The right-hand pair at 16 works through 17, 18, 19, 20, 21, down to 25 and is left.

(12) The pair left at pin 16 works out to 22, back to 23, then 24 and works down to 25. Make a whole stitch with the pair hanging from 21. Make a whole stitch, pin up at 25 and cover the pin.

The above method describes the movements of the threads without the complications of twists.

In the second sample, two twists have been added between each pair of passives and three twists have been added in the spaces between the lines of passives.

The next exercise is to reduce the scale of the pricking by half. This will reduce the width to 1.5 cm. The dots are then 4 cm apart along the straight edge. No. 100 crochet cotton is needed on the bobbins.

Working with beads

Beads are threaded on to the cotton before winding the bobbin. Insert folded florist's wire through the bead first. Pass a bobbin through the loop in the wire and then pull the cotton back through the bead. A second bobbin is inserted through the loop formed and the bead is then incorporated into the pattern (figs. 23, a, b and c).

'Fishing Net'. A lampshade ring has been used as a frame, and is worked in Sylko perlé 5 and 8 in cloth stitch and plaits (Janet Gross).

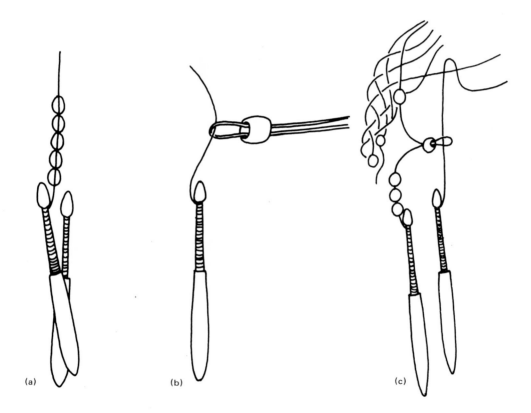

(a)　　(b)　　(c)

Fig. 23 (a, b, c). Working with beads.

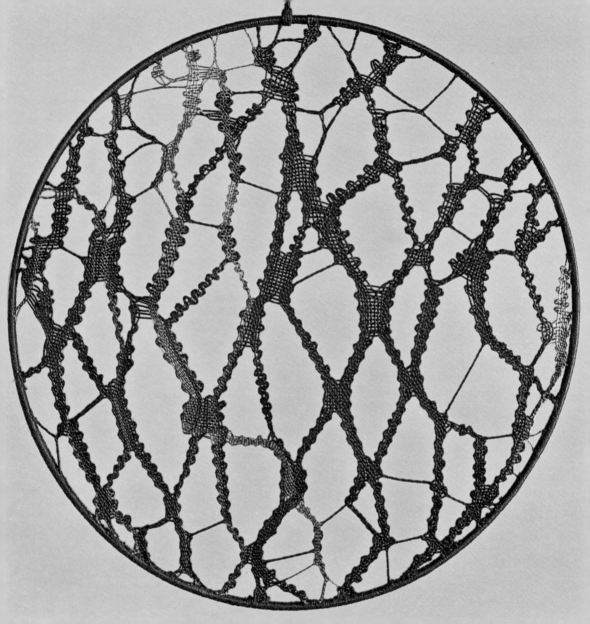

Gimp threads

These can be woven under and over the threads of the background in such a way as to outline a design or motif in a pattern (fig. 24). Traditionally, the thread used was a heavier weight and usually shiny white.

In creative work the threads may be run in a different colour from that of the background.

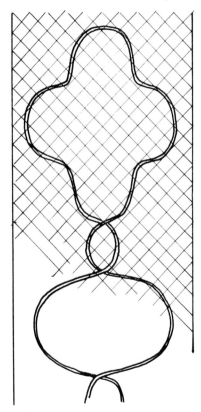

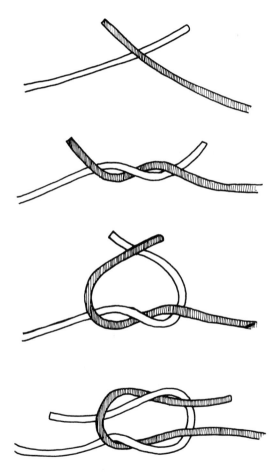

Fig. 24. Using gimp threads to outline a design.

Fig. 25. A reef knot.

Broken threads

Broken threads can be joined with either a reef knot (fig. 25) or a weaver's knot (fig. 26). Carry on working until the knot gets in the way, then place a pin to the outside of the pattern, twist the thread with the knot around the pin, take the bobbin back into the work and continue with the lace. The knot can be cut off when the work is finished.

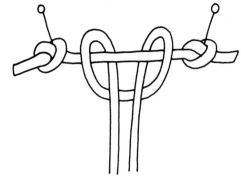

Fig. 27. A simple hitch.

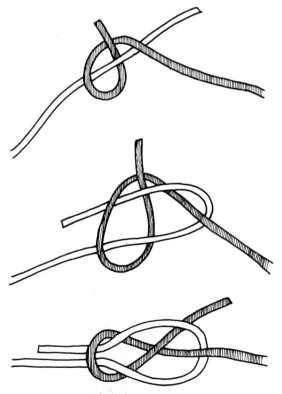

Fig. 26. A weaver's knot.

Creative lace

Up to now, there have been a set number of bobbins hung on pins with a pattern to follow. For creative work it may be necessary to hang bobbins into a shape, such as a circle. To do this, bobbins can be attached to a cord or ring by a simple hitch as shown in fig. 27.

After lace-making

When not being worked, the bobbins should be held down on the pillow with a length of ribbon or elastic. Cover the pillow with a cloth to keep it free from dust.

To wash lace that has become dirty, lay it in a saucepan with detergent and warm water and bring it to the boil. Leave it to soak for a short time, then rinse in cool water. Wrap the lace in a towel to get rid of excess water. Do not wring or twist it. Pin it into shape on the ironing board, lay a cloth over it and iron.

Acknowledgments

Edited by Kit Pyman

Text by Nenia Lovesey

Diagrams by Jan Messent

Text, illustrations, arrangement and typography copyright © Search Press Limited 1979.

First published in Great Britain in 1979 by Search Press Limited, 2-10 Jerdan Place, London SW6 5PT.

ISBN 0 85532 414 7

Made and printed in Spain by Editorial Elexpuru Hnos, Zamudio-Bilbao.

Frontispiece:

Wedding crown. Worked in crochet cotton 100 (Catherine Barley).

Edging for wedding veil and crown. Worked in sewing thread, this edging is formed by scaling down the pricking for the simple insertion from the one-inch width. The scallop effect is achieved by drawing both pairs of workers tight before and after the working of the centre pin. The crown edging uses the same pricking but with one pair of bobbins on the inside edge of both sides wound with a thicker thread, such as 100 crochet cotton. (Nenia Lovesey).

Back cover:
Left: Bedfordshire lace. A typical piece worked in ecru thread no. 100 (Nenia Lovesey).

Centre: 'Angel'. A creative design worked from a sketch on squared-paper in 80 crochet cotton (Carol Townsend).

Right: A fine Torchon edging. A shell-pattern edge with a hay stitch base in no. 60 cotton using 16 pairs of bobbins (Dorothy Handley).